THE WOMAN WHO LOVED WORMS

and other poems

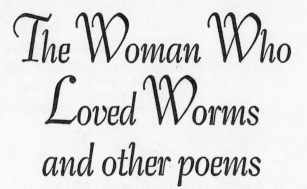

The Woman Who Loved Worms

and other poems

COLETTE INEZ

1972
DOUBLEDAY & COMPANY, INC., GARDEN CITY, NEW YORK

Some of these poems appeared in the following publications:
COLD DUST OF VESTMENTS, *New Canadian & American*,
No. 6, Copyright © 1968 by John Gill; WERE TWO, AM ONE,
Perspective, Copyright © 1968 by Perspective, Inc.; WHEN I
WAS SOFT AS FERNS, *Quartet*, Copyright © 1966 by Quartet;
MURDERING NUMBERS, *Poetry Northwest*, Copyright ©
1970 by Poetry Northwest; PLANES OF THE REPUBLIC,
GREENLAWN DAYS, *Hyperion Poetry Journal*, Copyright ©
1971 by Judith Hogan and Paul Foreman; MOVIE MANAGER,
Mediterranean Review, Copyright © 1971 by Robert De Maria;
LOOKING FOR MY MOTHER, OZARK LOVE, EMPRESS
IN THE MIRROR, and NILDA, AS GOOD NEWS, NILDA
IS BACK, *The Little Magazine*, Copyright © 1971, 1970, 1969
by The Little Magazine; MEETING IN LONDON, *Seneca Review*, Copyright © 1970 by Seneca Review; DR. INEZ, *Antaeus
1971*; JUNKYARD DEATH, *Prairie Schooner*; DAYS AND
PEACHES, ON FIRST USING PURPLE, *The Small Pond*;
FOR NANA, *Epos*; OLD LADY ACROSS THE HALL, *South
Dakota Review*, Copyright © 1967 by University of South Dakota;
BLINDNESS OF BLOOD, *Ante*, Copyright © 1968 by Ante-
Echo Press, solely owned by Vera Hickman; FORCE OF SNOW,
Shenandoah; BLUE GOWN'S ALICE, ATOMIC BLAST IN
THE BARNYARD, *Poet Lore*, Copyright © 1967 by Literary
Publications Foundations, Inc.; LASTVISIT, *Voices International*,
Copyright © 1967 by South and West, Inc.; HURTLED DOWN
TO FATHOM LOVE, *The Smith #8*, Copyright © 1968 by The
Smith; MUSCATEL, *Poet 1967*; ANNIVERSARY, *Motive*, Copyright © 1969 by Board of Education of the Methodist Church;
COLD WALTZES, SHAH OF THE TUNDRA, *The Nation*;

FOR SAUL

Contents

I

Corridors

Processionals

Peachstones

II

Cables

Hustings

Dybbuks

Orchards

I write to survive the darkness by signaling my light, for music, celebration, wordlove, the interpretation of experience, to say people are unique as each snowflake in its palace of light melts but is never lost, to intensify as a telescope gives the moon back to our eyes enlarging us with craters, basalt dust and time.

It is the beginning and the middle for me. The beginning because I started late, late to love, marry, craft poems. On good days I feel new, a fresh blue coat in my morning, white galaxies on apple skin as I bite into the core, snowflakes in the radish slice, sharp perceptions, cables in the grass. Middle because that's where chronology pins me, at the outer edge of my thirties, wearing my face like an unlaced shoe, nice all the same, knowing no repairman will redo it. Got used to the seams when I was a floorwalker in the world, a light bulb in my rib cage turned on or defused according to events.

I look forward, in a way, to being old, another kind of passion, to be less slovenly with time, compressed, to deepen like a cedar house, weathered outside, warm within, and foundering by degrees into the ground. But I dread the world I will be aging in; the history of greed, glut, exploitation of the weak by those in power probably to continue and increase. Heavy boots. Shriek of missiles. Privacy loss. Respectable men in council rooms sanctifying murder.

I am not detached. The procession of young faces, slayers and victims both, passes along my TV screen like a monstrous cortege: babies at My Lai, Ivans in their tanks bulldozing Czechoslovakia, the skeletons of Biafra, penned in ghettos, children of the kingdoms of Benin, migrant workers stoop laboring and defeated in the richest republic of all time. Kent State. Jackson. Impotent rage. Mine. It goes into my poems. Yet I don't figure on dying before my everything has become collapsible forms.

In THE WOMAN WHO LOVED WORMS are divisions that tell, in part, of my journey from a "quarter moon . . . refractory and white" to "lovers, hot with quarreling and tears." Childhood's parade and rituals of growing flow through "Corridors" and "Processionals." "Peachstones" portrays women, their passions buried like stones that once bore fruit. Telegrams from the headlined cry of cities, "parishes of crime," the feast and famine of my "brothers and sisters who walk the world" are in "Cables." Exiled souls rove in "Dybbuks." And while "Hustings" explores imaginary countries of the mind, "Orchards" holds known love as "an Ozark banjo twanged by the sun" flares into song if you listen.

THE WOMAN WHO LOVED WORMS

and other poems

I

Corridors

A Collar Rounds My Thought

Priest, my father, priest,
your collar cuts my neck,
my resonating breath's
intake
at knowing you were naked,
the collar jettisoned,
a crescent on the floor
where the bed upheld
my mother's pity for your sex.
Your strict lips kissed
her thirty years of fear,
kissed them away,
her dainty bones
under your own
barely moving
like the quarter moon
lighting the room,
like the tightening collar
caught in the light
choking desire
in the penitent hours
before my birth.
Priest, my father, priest,
your collar rounds my thought
like a moon, refractory and white.

Latin scholar, library dust
on your face, glossing tomes
next to her breath.
Only intellect
before her flesh
set your loins on edge.
Then transfixed,

desiring her
as the lame desire miracles.
Two scholars at dusk.
Not Heloise nor Abelard,
neither their youth
nor calamitous love.
Priest, my father, priest,
your collar rounds my world
like an equator
burning to know your life
interred forever in that faith
which primed your guilt.
No stigma on the grave,
only your name witnessed by rain
and I, your bastard child.

Cold Dust of Vestments

Cold dust of vestments
where my father stood
in the mottled light
of the sacristy

fastening his cassock
over a soul
astounded with lust.

Women: balm for his fever
tipped from their skin.
In his lightest dream
their hands like myrrh

scenting his temples
far from the weight
of the church.

Were Two, Am One

Sperm fathered
my thrust
into the vault
of a friendly bank.
Womb mothered my stay,
deeded its slick
upholstery.
A fund of solace
in the safety box.

Late, I sprang
the lock,
pitched my share
of Papa's loot
to starving clerks,
seduced the teller
and put on file
mother's unevicting
smile
for later.

Infant Ward

Heads of cabbage in the cribs
daily watered in a row,
I hear their pale green screaming,
a unison of pain,
and recognize my own,
a dirty garden in the bed,
the shaking out of residue.
Vegetable nights in the infant ward,
hosed down in darkness,
our rolling hearts,
corpuscular, arranged in rows,
a spasm in our runny veins,
strangling milk
inside our throats,
we cried to be human
in the image of Him
who suckled stars in Bethlehem.

Looking for My Mother

My mother vanished like a rabbit in a sleazy act,
red-eyed, perplexed, chomping words in an exiled coop.
Soft, primed with incantation, believed her Mandrake,
his palpable cape flowing like the sky, full of cures,
the miraculous church, cathedrals of illusion,
a trunk of props and optical tricks.

I will look for her in multicolored scarves the light
gives out, through secret pockets of a town that held her heart,
in the weather's coolness at the rim of the sky
where she roomed each night applauding the stars.

I will look for her in the archives of rabbits,
missing Belgian, prairie, arctic hares, a computation
of unlucky rabbits, more details than I care to note.

I care to note her stunned, long glance prey
to the Predator Magician who drugged her leaping into love,

will seek her out in porkpies, derbies, straws,
her pink dreams shadowed in their brims,
and if I find her, will stroke her fur
in the regular assemblies and sad, dumb shows
for brats without rabbits or ABRA-SHAZAM
doorways to mother's most excellent love.

Orphans of All Denominations Will Meet
(*From a sign in the 96th Street subway*)

Orphans of all denominations will meet
in Tierra del Fuego orphanage grounds
near the sign that says:
>   Do Not Step on the Orphans
>   Do Not Smoke the Orphans

they've been burned enough
in the sizzling lake that shines like the smile
of Razzle Bath the sleuth man.

Orphans of all denominations will meet in Heidelberg
near the autobahn sign that says:
>   Achtung!
>   Do Not Pick the Orphans

from out of the grass where they memorize lice on the pillows.

Buddhist, Shinto, Bahai, Seventh Day, Animist orphans
will meet in Mali near the airport sign that says:
>   Check All
>   Orphans
>   With the
>   Baggageman

and buckle them in to dream of passage like doomed geese
stunned with corn and gorged for the feast of organs.

Orphans of all remunerations, 50-cent orphans, living wage orphans,
minus-the-price-of-abortion orphans will meet
in Valdosta near the sign that says:

                              Put an Orphan in Your Tank
and see the longer miles he smiles in the speed of forgetting
orphanage picnics the empire packs in throwaway time.

Be nice to the orphans. They want to suffer shipshape lives
in our ribald state which is dying in all denominations
near the sign that says:
                              No Disrobing Orphans on the Beach;
offenses will be met on orphanage grounds—
disposable minds and redeemable whips
free to the keeper of orphans.

Processionals

When I Was Soft as Ferns

When I was soft as ferns around the roses,
I sang processionals at morning service
and rode my gladness high on backyard swings.
Hummed alto to every hymn the choir knew,
but in the fields and weeds I grew
with sticks and stones and hurting things.

And now when morning comes and night is over,
I, having fought the terrors from all corners
of hours soaked in brimming darkness,
arise and limply hang my questions
on rusted hooks that streak the naked wood,
and then a tired knowing strokes me
with answers in my secret blood.

Orphans at the Iron Gate

Stone was younger under the clogs of Mijnheer Walloon
tightly-buttoned and mulling. Air was calmer—
old domino Ursuline nun gliding on cobbles.
Death milder, monastic larder bare at dusk,
black monk's dogma slumbering
when I was smaller than the altar where I knelt
like a flutter at the Eucharist.

Drifting past the junipers, feebly singing
convent girls crowd my ear with names: Chantal, Cécile,
Jeanine, Sylvie. We were those the bishop heard
blurred inside the choristers' pale "Sanctus,"
orphans at the iron gate, fed on bells and curdled light.

I pave with dreams the corridors that walked my sleep,
my waking hours, shrunk my body to a voice
pounding for reasons behind the church's bolted door.
Days like cowls of Carmelite, medieval, frayed.
Wednesday ashes scattering the pious years my mind denied.
Anemic answers slowed my blood. Phantasmal flesh
and ikons of Jesus, his plaster smile spurring my love.

Now love is older under the hum of pollen, Belgian summer
of phlegm and rain. Spartan grass at the fading gate.
The ritual of light and dark tolling on the children;
in a cancelled time, my counterparts, orphaned but luxuriant,
exhaling loss in their iron cribs.

Murdering Numbers

Soissy-sur-École, unstintingly French,
have been there with a plow
tilling numbers and non-numbers
in the school rain, smudged arithmetic,
problems in chalk; dowdy captive to a desk,
and chained to mademoiselle's voice,
the gusseted serge of her proper dress.

Rain-glyphs on the windowpane;
I tried to break the code, assured that the script
opened locks to a drenched world
of storm kings, cloud queens, thunderous bosoms,
that lightning bid the populace
to cower in their huts
until a prince was found for the princess:
rain-droplet eyes, white tulip breasts,

but was ferruled into fractions,
mutilated digits, numbers on the chopping-block,
dissected in half and less than whole,
the unwholesome practice of minus signs,
these wounded ciphers less than
those decapitated ones. A hospital of numbers,
slashed, crippled, hobbling on the blackboard.

The land outside the room
luminously plus in the lavender light.
It was where I wanted to count froth, grass,
inconsequentially dazzling leaves reading the rain,
inimical to grocery lists, recipes halved,

bank interest and loans, things that math was good for
in the gray-serge freshly ironed town where I was from,

but stayed after school, the rain-script erased,
memories of rain stored in the chalk.
In the chalk-dust room I slaughtered fractions,
my diagonal knife's stab-stab,
absurd reductions into air,
the globe I wrote on like the zero I would get
in Soissy-sur-École
when I was there
murdering numbers.

Smear of Beetles in a Jar,
Our Homefront Effort Towards the War

Smashing the Axis, we raided the shrub,
imagining Tojo's jaundiced smile,
Kamikaze pilots,
yellow daubs across the map,
hula-hula islands in our geography
of unpronounceable names.

The Warden told us: beetles,
foreign, stealthy feet,
were attacking the spine
of American leaves.

Bare hands to snare the beasts,
their pitchblend backs like licorice
in the mayonnaise jar.

Routinized terror.
We drowned them in urine and flame
learning to love their failure to live.

The Planes of the Republic

purring above lawns, strips of billiard cloth
spinning my summer into pockets.

Tyranny in the heat,
a lightbulb screwed inside my skull
while giant mothers armed with spoons
scooped milk of magnesia down my throat,
saying it's alright.

Alright if I'd been a Grumman aircraft
rumbling over lots,
no neighbors to conjure my future:
idiot years I'd climb like a sloth,
glued-together dreams with unmoveable parts
staring headlong at the dark.

Alright if I'd been a Corsair in double formation
with a Grumman Goose, a lovely plane of the republic
thrumming ergo sum, my wings commuting from landstrips
to an aerodome heaven above the clouds.

Heaven, Harpo at its gate,
God, a retired pilot, accelerated angels
accepting my propellers, their blaze far from the hutch
where my body-life crouched
dreaming of the spin.

Movie Manager, Paris, France

L'Odéon, black cookie box
dotted with crumbs.
I'm propped inside
near a movie sky
that sings in French.

Suddenly, the volume's off.
Dialogue of sickness,
myself and my legs.
The lurching aisle
spills me into soundlessness.

Awake from collapse;
the movie manager's
rubbery hand
under my blouse.

Ah, merde. A jet of spit
from my pretzel mouth.
Saliva in his squat moustache.

His steaming eyes
like two fresh drops
of country dung,
enriching my pity,
fattening my rage.

Dreamskin

The vehicle,
a shamble
of cracked parts,
propelled from smoke
to the wounded wreck
of my body's dream,
the one I wore
for the swerve
night took.

I wake
careening into light.

And the skin of dreams
like scum,
a caul's thin slime,
clings to the morning.

My dreamskin yawns,
a hooded snake
essing into wakefulness;

this skull, its brittle den
in aftermaths of siren.

Meeting in London

That I leapt from her hips, her tidy legs soiled
with my cries into forceps; the looming nurse and intern,
masked bandits, rifling my mother's womb like a bank.

And from the steel-precision hospital, a Wermacht band,
I smartly marched, oompah . . . pah, Zieg Heil,
into Third Reichs of my childhood. Ya!

Now drab, brown hours in the silence, the sun,
a faucet dripping time, my mother a forest, winterwood:
birch and ravelling oak,
damp waves pinched along the neck,

her glances drifting on my lips, my face
reflecting dread, (she'd abandoned me, like Munich,
and trusted the regime).

I call her name across the rubble.
Achtung! You will love me,
the thought clicked heels,
though my Nazis float in a limbo of Jews
who turned in their own children.

Auf wiedersehen. One gold molar in her mouth,
the only gaudiness, device to memorize her smile
in the squeezed-out light, lemony and dry,
the sky over London in a bowler hat, palest gray, invisible.

Waiting for the Doctor

I hear the doctor's loud success
booming to the anteroom,
my convent girl legs
criss-crossed at the ankles
narrowing the chapel where love huffs
like a wolf in the gray light
of redemptive sex.
Eucharistic body, tasty wafer,
Bristol-Cream sherry tapping through my veins,
Catholic outcome of a priest-father,
medieval mother on the guest bed of the parish,
witnessed by an ivory angel
and a watercolor Christ.

Waiting for the doctor, his loud success,
I think: my mother's breasts at thirty
tightening in my father's palms,
a crack inside her plaster flesh
widening for life,
my infant body's instant flush.

Disgusting girl—female scum, dirty secretions
attendant on woman's time, my mother thought
tying the parcel to mail me away.
I, reared on the assembly line,
factory for molding children into nuns.
Orphanage cookie, my cookie-self

waiting for the doctor
to come and view my masterworks:

assemblages of bone, mid-symphysial stage of decay,
sculptures for love programmed to fail,
but doubling cells under my flesh humming like a laundromat,
a 9-lb. load to cart in and out of next year's bed.

Dr. Inez

I'm a resident, Dr. Inez, touring the wards.
These rooms I walk contain superb
examples of degenerate sorrow.
My instructors outline stages of decay
which they in turn excise,
bearing their trays of implements.
Blueplate cures and bogus hopes. Curettage.
Curés of cures.

The cold wind scrapes my eyes,
onward go the spectacles; cafeteria selections,
dishy, broad delectables, eggplant breasts, but
malignant eyes like tumors
spreading lies about my skill.

A chill. Autumn's critical condition.
Must I scrutinize the blood, urine, gangrene
in the leaves?
I, Dr. Inez, sincere, not yet coarsened by events,
circumnavigating pain, the hapless Lourdes of suffering,
amputee processionals to a light
some quack child dreams
fattening her father's coin at the bank.

Tomorrow's snow winds bandages.
I will confess to patched-up truths;
the press of wretchedness,
leprous fingers at my throat,
and must devise a better way
to stick like tape in a dampening room
before time's blade prepares to cut
the central valve to all I love.

Ballad to an Aborted Daughter

Won't she ride
the homing gull
in cobalt blue lagoons,

my daughter
blasted like a bridge
in Scranton, Pennsylvania.

Won't she dance
quadrilles
in porticoes of jessamine,

my daughter
full of chemicals
and blown to bits
in Scranton, Pennsylvania.

Won't she sing
beige lullabies
in lavender ravines

or fly to la Pamplona, Spain
to weep for bulls,

my daughter in the ring
which sealed my womb,
splintered by grenades
and nitroglycerine
in Scranton, Pennsylvania.

Won't she run
on a white snow road
dragging a sled downhill
to my voice

when I explain
the man, myself
in an endless ring of accidents . . .

blood and shrubs, the rain-sopped curbs
of Scrantons in the world.

Peachstones

Greenlawn Days
(For my foster grandmother)

She took me Saturdays on the Beeline bus,
past hick towns belching after lunch,
to the cemetery gate. Greenlawn days.

And said, "I always hated waste,"
clenching my arm like a prize,
her free hand nabbing rose bouquets,
miniature flags and picture frames,
a rheumy focus in her eyes
under the sky's farsightedness.

Sizing her plot, a scraggy mound,
viewed by mausoleums,
their popeyed angels hoisting scrolls,

she made me read the names, the proper dead,
blunted under sediment,
lulled by verses in the turning star
I hated for its slowness in making me grow.

Old woman, old woman, my shield and my wound,
I saw her grow frail in the stone of each sun,
hammered down to eighty years of blindness,
unreformed when the casket closed
and lowered to a stingy grave;

crabgrass and wasps squandering their poems,
common rhymes for a scavenger lady
I wanted to love.

Lastvisit

1.
Granny,
snarling incisors
tense ears,
huffed the carnations
smack to the floor,

voice grew claws
ripping my silence,
said: "They bring on
bugs, you fool." I was.

Horseflies dove
from the ceiling
double gainers
into the hour.

"I did my best,"
I said to her.
It was my old
defensive self
mewling for pity.

2.
I owned a hectare
in my dream,
carnations in silos,
a croft of spleen,

myself, a farmer
stalking the wolf
who tore my heifers,
crazed my mare.

Woke to find Granny
dogging my thought,
blood in the corners
of her mouth.

Days and Peaches

Pinching days and peaches,
she eked out a tune
in cutlery time
and swung on summer porches.

Elberta's best
turning to rot,
it defied her to slice
the cankers out,

preserve the good
in Mason jars
for nights the winters
chilled.

Peachstones buried
in the yard
refused to seed an orchard,
though spading rain
gardened hard,

while the blight in her
was too far ranged
for any scalpel.

For Nana

Came swagging her cane
through the garden
in thin-tongued witches' shoes.
Threatened the sun with her rages,

but he, being old, understood
the crooked bones of the venerable lady,
the hooded eye,
the clapboard breast.

He saw her lead the air,
baton to scare the tanagers,
kissed the folds along her neck,
her white barbed hair.

Then the lady sat,
cowed the grass beneath her haunches,
there among the fallen plums,
cursed the withering of love.

The Old Lady Across the Hall
Has Gone to Live Behind the Door

In a country of drifting spectacles
she flicks on the hours and dials the sun.
The track of time moves gray on gray;
her mind daubs in the colors,
converts a blurred announcer's eyes
to mauve chiffon, her aureole
when old beaux drove the Landaus down
macadam roads to home.
The screen explodes its Catherine Wheels
and spins her into yawning.
Transfixed, she twirls the starbox off.
Herself alone behind a door,
twiddling years on yellow thumbs
before a blur of furniture.

The Blindness of Blood

Could not feel
the socket of my hunger;
her own so great.

Stirred a past
she hoped would stick
flesh on my ribs.

Muffed her ears
against the slur
of words my tongue

pulled down to her,
tuned our life
to static.

And tapped a cane
in a maze
of scrubbed linoleum

dimly managing a braille
her mind declined
to master.

Blindness, blinder,
deafness more deaf.

I reached for singing
in myself
and tore down colors
from the world

to hoard when famine
struck.

Force of Snow

What went out
of the house
(refuse, smoke,
fumes of roast,

a hausfrau love
for placed things),

that ice grips
the mansard roof
contracts the frame
of a wizened door?

Inside, cold to colder
fires
soil the grate
she scrapes for heat.

The mansion's lady
sets the clock
to ring on summer;

green caved in
on porches,
pine branch sawing
down the light.

No hounding love
kept at bay,
howling rage
held back.

The force of snow
on the house, a weight
of dimming sense.

She hears her mind
unwinding
music from a dented horn

and lets things
come to rot.

Blue Gown's Alice

Blue Gown's Alice
(stored in a closet
in Greenlawn's cellared stone),
reclines a skeleton
that twirled
past medicines and cures.

A strut in clinic aisles
to orchestrated clocks,
wound to zero time
when interns failed to raise
the stepped-down pulse.

Danced the Big Apple of dying,
bruises pounding at the core.
Rolling her pulp
toward the fevered moon,
she called for one whirl more.

But sat out the dance in a casket
while mourners in black
reeled up and back
to curtsy their regret.

The Woman Who Loved Worms

(From a Japanese legend)

Disdaining butterflies
as frivolous,
she puttered with caterpillars,
and wore a coarse kimono,
crinkled and loose at the neck.

Refused to tweeze her brows
to crescents,
and scowled beneath dark bands
of caterpillar fur.

Even the stationery
on which she scrawled
unkempt calligraphy,
startled the jade-inlaid
indolent ladies,
whom she despised
like the butterflies
wafting kimono sleeves
through senseless poems
about moonsets and peonies;
popular rot of the times.

No, she loved worms,
blackening the moon of her nails
with mud and slugs,
root gnawing grubs,
and the wing case of beetles.

And crouched in the garden,
tugging at her unpinned hair,
weevils queuing across her bare
and unbound feet.

Swift as wasps, the years.
Midge, tick and maggot words
crowded her haikus
and lines on her skin turned her old,
thin as a spinster cricket.

Noon in the snow pavilion,
gulping heated saki
she recalled Lord Unamuro,
preposterous toad
squatting by the teatray,
proposing with conditions,
a suitable marriage.

Ha! She stoned imaginary butterflies,
and pinching dirt,
crawled to death's cocoon
dragging a moth to inspect
in the long afternoon.

II

Cables

Listening With My Feet

Sewerpipes fluting, copulating rats,
the drain's death-rattle,
manhole's dreaming out loud
of Proserpine,
her journey to the bowels of Hell.

rotgut sighing in broken flasks,
rasping gutters mouthing pulp,
steel tunes of warnews, ho-humming
cables,

a sidewalk's moaning migraine,
the curb's cracked cough,
alliterative stones singing
chanties for the dead,
trapdoors eating beggars,
the blistered voice of ruined men.

Hearing with my feet,
I learned chorales,
hosannahs to the damned,
my brothers and my sisters
who walk the world.

Slumnight

T.V. gunning down
the hours
serves as sheriff
in a room
where one yawn
triggers off another,

sends time scuffling
into night.
Wars slugged out
on vacant lots
sign an armistice
with sleep.

Turned to a wall,
the children dream
and the moon pulls up
in a squadcar.

Priest

Umbrella's collapse of ribs and silk.
Accordion folds, the busdoor bangs,
takes the man into its song: gears,
brakes, horn, melodic grooves
of road and curb turning his trammeled
brainwaves

which gloss the grandnesses of God,
gold-plated crozier, monstrance in a church
padlocked against hoodlums,
their avatars at Golgotha
when the nails were driven in.

The priest descends to snapping rain,
bar and grill neon green on his skin,
abrading collar and crucifix,
a crumbling Bible and his belief
short of mercy, funds for love.

God's gutturals in a parish of crime;
the stammering sky thunders him home
to a vandalized altar and smashes of wine
on the gutter's lip, in the sneering streets
where Angels are gangs
who would mug Christ if he lived.

Remembering the Dances

She died of cirrhosis and was laid out
on a marble lounge, pickled-beet dark lips
tasting taffeta and salt.

He went on unplugged, dragging his cord
like a telephone, out-of-order, vandalized,
remembering the dances: Lambeth Walk, the Shag, the Truck.

Nevermind the gin-blurred drives
to any dive the turnpike flashed.

Remembering the dances.
Five fundamental steps to quickened bliss
on the Arthur Murray Plan.

Turkey Trot and Lindy Hop
blotting up the raw egg light of morning.

Remembering the dances smooth as frozen daiquiris,
dipping straws in the world's chilled glass.

Nevermind the crumpling legs after the dances,
flesh too etherized to speak.
Money's rumba swung their hips
swizzling the Conga, Mambo, Argentine Tango.

Dancing to remember the dances.
Dancing to remember not dancing
was formaldehyde, syringe bags of blood.
No Irene Castle in the afterworld of shut down bars.

"One more drinkee" for the floating road
that reeled inside the ward. Tapping stars
in the ballroom sky, Cugat's throb and plush, big bands
remembering

she was his party favor,
freshly pleated and hoorayed,
whiskeys away, martini standard time
in the foxtrot lounge of yesterdays.

Packing his attachments like a vacuum-cleaner man,
he sells the goods to anyone, even himself
in the closing hours after her death
and takes a belt of rye to sweep aside
all the steps they took in between the dances.

Good News! Nilda Is Back

Good news! Nilda is back,
the sign huzzahs
in the Beauty Shoppe

as the rain combs
the sky over and over
like a grandmother combing
the hair of a child.

Impermanent waves
of rain on the street;
the trees are straight
but the city bends.

Nilda is back
from Guayaquil,
Quito, Ponce,
San José

to tease the gringo smiles
of blue-eyed wives
in the raining city.

And now she cha chas up the aisles
to supervise the upswept lines
of an aging lady

who does not know why Nilda comes
or why she goes
or where her hair uncurls at night
damp at the edge from waves of love.

On First Using Purple
(For *Juan Echevarría*)

Echevarría turned
a stumpy knob of crayon
and was purple's despot
ruling over white,
made his color trek
through the landscape of himself.

His tyranny of lavender,
short and blunt,
yet altered the calendar,
the log of his trip,

when he, Echevarría,
scaling worlds of plum,
was conquistador of reaches
distant to his slum.

Mrs. Maldonado's Daughter

Plump as a scallop, she pounds on the piano,
organdy dress, puffed sleeves,
puffed little breasts,

while Mama stoops in the tailor shop,
pinching cloth, pleating darts,
basting hems for customers on Broadway
with poignant necks and dropped behinds
all exacting large demands.

Mrs. Maldonado's gold at home, bon bon girl,
marshmallow skin, socially good
like the milky fingers beringed in amethyst
plunking on the keyboard.
Pink velvet lips pressed to a shine,
her child, she thinks, thank god,
not dark like a roasted chestnut
steaming in the street.

She will play "Malagueña" and "Tico Tico"
for every Sunday's company,
fed on sugared water, chocolate squares,
marzipan bananas and mounds of rice.

Mrs. Maldonado's daughter swelling like a sail
on an ivory sea of musical selections
will pump off-key and billow
until the day, like pinking shears,
points to Mama's curry skin,
and a dusty machine where the money was sewn,

green sashes of it to bind the girl's flesh:
Quality Merchandise. Instrument: Piano.
No Men of Color Need Apply

for the only daughter of Señora Maldonado,
light as farina and sired
in the dark, lattice-work nights
of romantic San Juan.

Junkyard Death
(For our piano)

Yellow teeth clenched
into black gums.
Roped, strapped,
dangling over concrete,
now the hulk of her goes down,
hoisted to a sour morning.

Once she bellowed
in this room,
whole note rumps swayed
and fingers mumbled songs
along her body.

Plunked down the years,
blitzed on boogie and jazz;
we pumped her full
of boozy smiles
before the lid slammed shut.

The tow truck dumps her
into death;
junkyard's grime
astounding her mouth.
Our silence, a warehouse
of worn down loves,
recalls her stoutness
rounding our nights
before we cracked,
divorced (off-pitch),

pledges to honor
banged in our face,
tone-deaf walls
straining for music.

A Mind's Sad Order Serves the Air

In the Medical Center luncheonette
a man said: "Everything is leaving;
women in rabbit-persian-bear-skunk coats,
rainbow brains, hands from their gloves,
money from its folds,

buses and hollering trains, breath into words,
youth in our cells, birds for the south.
Even the stars moving to the rim of the universe,
their streamers waving adios.

When I pay this check
I will leave and drop my face at the end
of a van, my teeth escaping from their roots,
my buckling gums, and this insanely bleeding suit
to give up its veins.

Disposed as a grapefruit leaves its rind
like a child from its mother's lap
for the infirm school and nailed-down desks
that will leave.
The principal's curlicued smile
processed to a straight line
that will leave
its replica in photographs that will crack and brown
like an Okie farm leaving soil to the wind in its Will
that will leave
me and my sound's balloon trailing to the door
that helps me leave
for the world's peak where clouds guzzle light
like a lush that was my father not speaking

and leaving
with his new 6-pack, an invisible valise
spilling out the crud, and ersatz thoughts
he clung to,
drab accumulations, unrefunded bonds
that left before I zipped my fly
and waved goodbye to greetings
from lips that closed like midtown bars
at four o'clock, nothing on the house in closing eyes
that leave their sight to darkness.

Everything is oracles
that will leave this tip intact. Formica counters
inching away back of the glass while I stay
leaving my chair always displaced and away where I sat."

Collapsible Forms

Madonna of cream flannel ski suits after snow,
Mandarin nails, raspberry fire tapping boredom
like the blind at curbs,

no message coming through your ultra-purple lips,
lipstick eating teeth slurring British vowels
at local dives where teamsters eyed your cleavage
as if it were a turnpike in the dark.

After the fifth Cuba Libre, uproarious companions
who drained the mugs and slobbered
unblotted love like dirty rain.

Dark frontiers in your hennaed hair:
that passageway to your brainwaves clogged.

I slumped in your sight like Achilles' tent
(when he entered downhearted with the war).
Your coldness was colossal then—
Antarctica at twilight calling zero from its depths.

Now I see your face unopened, blowing on the slopes,
an envelope with no address, dying letters
of your name.

The flannel ski suit in time's debris, sirloin for moths,
gone like our lives to collapsible forms.

For Denise McNair
(Bombed in Birmingham, Alabama, September 15, 1963)

Testified that Miss McNair
on an Alabama Sunday
in the colored church,
the reverend saying:
"Evil and good share
God's light"
when the pews blew up,
walls caved, ceiling crashed,

did hereupon
plunge down
to the brown earth
having learned her testament:
the meek inherit dust.

Okapi

Congo fawn, thin-lidded
and slatted behind,
he rolls towards a depth of mahogany,
liana vine a foothold
in the banded darkness

and dreams a lion
mincing through savannahs,
the great blond croup sashaying
under a sun whose rays mirror
the beast's ruff.

The lion pawing gourds
at roots of a Baobab,
where he, the okapi
stands by him as a brother
licking the skin of the moss.

Basutos

Basutos weave
straw roofs
that move
in Afrikaaner sleep.

And the sleepers'
ken of darkness
looms
under a tusk of moon.

Deep the mine of sleep
embedded in a hut
where Bantus scoop
the diamond sweat

of Afrikaaner heat.

Afrikaaner heart
stunted in its flesh
clocks the swelling dread.

Down the pit of rage
black men gauge
their dynamite!

Amazon

". . . Brazil's leading social historian estimates that by 1980 the Indian population will be completely extinct." DIE ZEIT, *Hamburg*

A grip of orchids in the forest jaws,
and moaning lianas
caught in the morning fog of gauze
and the waking river.

Tribesmen sang to the cayman river, to the toucan river.
It was their mother straddling the moon, riding the water.
Amazon.

Tribal songs now clot in the throat,
silenced by embezzlers, and the "fazandeiro"
from his throne of guns. Blasted kingdoms
where Xingus thrived knowing no word for "punishment."

"Corte de baneiro," backward and forward swing of the blade,
slice of two heads in a single thrust,
and "corte maior" cleaving the tribesman
into two or more parts to thud on the ground—
blood jerking like a palsied snake to the river's pit.
Warrior river. Mourner of tribesmen.

Great sister-bird, the Cessna, vomiting bombs
while in the forest a girl hangs down, legs tied apart
as a rubber tapper chops her in half.

Huitoto, Crao, Ticuna men,
the river turns its cobbled skin
like a white city in the moon.
Green-plumed river, cayman of water,
mirror to the sun's blazing ribs of light.
At night, the land's mouth, emerald thirst,
spiked teeth and tongue in the marmoset's scream
taking the river into its dream,
exhaling water. Amazon.

Hustings

Postscript in the Snow

Our fence doesn't hear the grades of snow,
town a graph but minus lines,
a frowning hill of calomine.

Our fence doesn't hear the streets go still,
Dutch canals in a German dream, wooden thoughts
and slotted ears boxed by shrill, abusive years.

Only the archerbird, her arrows lost,
listens for signs; lovers in the iron church,
carnations in power and hustings of joy.

Deaf to mongers and aging squalls, proposing
to the archerbird they stay out the cold,
our fence in the snow didn't hear the aerials
warming for leaves, the passage of the archerbird
when no signs came.

Atomic Blast in the Barnyard

The goosegirl screams
as the silo cracks
as the sun hurls down
on the swirls of geese.

See the goosegirl run
with a goose and a hen
to the end of the lawn
as the wall falls down
as the hollyhocks snap
as the dead fowls flap
in the goosegirl's lap.

Sauerkraut Talk Shreds in His Ear

Sauerkraut talk shreds in his ear;
the night supine and breaking wind.
Chekov's "Life is cabbages and quarrels"
comes to mind
and how years growled
in time's distended stomach.

Flo at the end of the table
riffling through old recipes,
how her titties once were snow peas,
hair buttery, pepper-firm ass . . .

even the world was firmer
when they rolled through escaroles of summer
curled in the heart of the leaves.

Space Cage Poem I

I want to centipede
this space
with dark footsteps,
the thud
of an emperor insect
unmarked but there
in his compost realm
of roots and bark.

Climbing the redwood
of my mind
which holds a bird,
a lobbing bee,
smashes of aphid, drone
and midge,
the enemy zone
my ground grows in,

I want to intercede
this space
with light starfalls,
or the crash
of a Jovian sun
in its stellar realm
of turn and flame.

Climbing the bedrock
of my mind
which holds a bride,
a sobbing tree,
smashes of rancor, stodge

and love,
the enemy zone
my ground grows in,

I want this space
to centipede
the thud
of a Mandarin insect,
dark but there,
my counterpart
in the hammered air
of the enemy zone
my ground grows in.

Space Cage Poem II

Rye dreams
the heartland
with baffles of snow.

Overall, snow
unsettles the ruts
of our waking and sleep,

usurps the weather
cast in our mind,

forcing white
on miles we ride in.

Somewhere at the rim of snow

sorghum dreams
marauding crows
buried in snowfall
lose their blackness.

It is so to all our answers.
Snow.

Better to Spit on the Whip
Than Stutter Your Love Like a Worm

Better to spit
on the whip
that drives you
to dead work
where lashing clocks
will welt your back

than rot flint-hearted,
venomous and squat
like senators of war,
old men cloaked in wisdom
stuttering their love.

Honey Money Loves

Their rowdy mouths eating her gelt,
wampum, mazuma, cowries and cash,
long green, debentures, clinkers and wads.

Bloodsucking teeth in the smiles of her callers
tipping sombreros, serapes and pails
to scoop up the moola.

Peeling it off her back like adhesive,
bloated with loot they crawl down the slope
of her mountainous jack.

Mestizo eyes deep in the field
blazing like greed in the murderous green
of the money.

She'd strafe them down with counterfeit
but hoards her pain to stay alive
the rage,

and studs her life with gluttonous louts,
coveys of wheedlers, coaxers and oafs,
all gorging the money.

Dybbuks

Empress in the Mirror

With high-jewelled hair
the empress in the mirror
dallies:

jars of wax, powder, cotton,
kohl and rouge,
chessmen in a game of beauty.

Floating her pen on linen paper,
ink flying into wings of script,

that empress mocks my workday bones
which close me as a shutter
darkens the room of an invalid girl,

and sips my light while I scrape stones
for priestly secrets,
my eyes in their hoods like drunken monks

dreaming wine, monastic love,
arcane parchments where abbeys moved
their cauldrons for a fiendish lord.

My knees more ridged than a drudge's face,
her eloquent legs.

Imprisoned in my mirror, that empress says:
"I am to you as onyx is to gravel,"
pelting words to small enclosures
in my skull.

The Shah of the Tundra

The shah of the tundra
white in his kingdom of seal,
shrieking for harlots at midnight,

weeping in ermine at noon.
No vizir in his palace,

and love in an infidel country
far from caliph.   Silence!
Caribou advance

to hear the polar sultan
reciting the Koran.

The Rape of Arethusa

She races her life's
unstifled green
(her freedom
still at large)

against a man
who's shouting
he's a god,
who gains the wind
she needs to run.

Her thighs,
lean as a sprinter,
buckle and spread;
he prods.

But love, the quarry
gone.
Her body's triumph
cool as stone.

Baal Shem Tov

In a forest hovel words of the Cabala
wound him in a ring of dances;
bearded shadows flailing dust,
the bride, a cloud of flour
milling in the feast.

He leavened a dream. A wedding of joy
to joy, of joy to men!
Joy! It rose from his marrow
like the odor of challah
wafting angels in his hut.

Joy! His being became Baal Shem,
a name to soothe ghettos
stooped in darkness where dybbuks leapt
through walls of flesh.

And the fiddler whetted his strings,
the menfolk danced in rings
as the word of Baal Shem Tov
moved famine to feast, meanness to love.

Praise him, servant of God.

Zoroaster
(Killed by soldiers while at prayer)

Zoroaster
in the mosque
filled its crevices
with light,

lengthened it
with prayer
until it bloomed
with terror.

Crippled shadows
hid the knives
soldiers held
to gash

Zoroaster's blinding flesh.
Ground to sand
the shining mind.

Ahura Mazda,
shine upon our innocence.

Mercedes, Her Aloneness

1.

Her stiffening captor lies in wait
under the fronds of the palmetto.
Hamhock hands
arc to her breasts,
rennet mounds beneath a shift
of tapioca flowers.

2.

Give in, the heron creaks,
wing span greater than hands.
Go under,
below your heart the billowed waves.

3.

She goes. Mercedes bending wide-honed thighs
under the rawness of his hide.
Swimming the dusk with clogged ears,
salt in her nostrils.
Day's junk plumbing oblivious seas.

They spread the rhythm of their instant
over grit, stammering neon, veins
of asphalt hardening lawns
of balconied motels.

4.

Home. Sperm lashing her womb.
Lips pressed to the moon's
pole of wash on the shingled wall.

Doorslam's jolt. Muslin bind of sleep.
Crumpling flesh
dents the hour
with weights of breath.

5.
The air crawling on all fours
secreting its slime into her pores,
in the singular print of her palm,
anointing aloneness.

Queen Tiy's Assent

Fade fade
the faint mastaba
and the heron's stance

Salt on the moon
invaders from the south
braying slaves and mandrils
glazed in the flood
of disorderly war

while Tiy assents
to love her lord
wiping honey from his lips
the wind's cool linen
on her face

Raw birds in the air
Ammon's archers on the plain
a darkness festering in the sun

while Tiy
wiping honey from her lips
the wind's cool linen
assents to love
salt on the moon
braying slaves
to love her lord

Fade fade
Seti's head carved on a jar
runnels of gold
glazed in blood
the wind's cool moon
disorderly lips
Ammon's archers
hunting the sun
for Tiy to love
like a festering lord

Orchards

Dream Rungs of Z, the 26th Shore

On dream rungs of Z,
cocooned in a void,
the alphabet's end,
I'm sleeping Z.
No one's slept it yet
but me at the inclining door
                    of Z-zither, one stringed,
                        Z-mute swan
in the weather for mailing letters.
I will mail you Z for Zonelight as you move,
triple Z's trapped in a balloon,
mimicking the afterlove
                    of Z-zinger
                        Z-zonked
                        Z-the keen-nosed man
responding to a steeply-breasted woman,
her tilting like a graph
charting climates of Zowie, Zap.

You speak in Zanzibari, love,
zinc dust in your lungs.
But I've zoomed
to dream rungs of Z, a climb to zippered silence,
illiterate space
enclosing the zero my hasty face makes
floating from love.

Hurtled Down to Fathom Love

Iron reveries of dusk
seep inside
the dwindling room.

Skin on skin
revolves our flesh,
grafts another me

to him.
Dove's blue eyelids,
hair geranium.

Purely nude
the tolling breasts
chiming hours at his ear.

Plumped in glory
my body moves,

hurtles down
to fathom love.

In the Muscatel Afternoon

In the muscatel afternoon
with the sun swinging on the flesh of things,
there on the verge of the hill,
astride a palomino

you rode to the arbor.
Under a cypress, the wind ladling dust,
my breasts turned
suddenly hard.

Out of the north a chilled
pitch of geese against the sky,
the wild mistral's icy prod
shocking vineyards from their lull.

Breaking his post, the pony charged,
veered you toward the hill.
I saw you shriveled to a blot,
the whip of darkness at your back.

Anniversary

Far   begins at any moment;
each then was the time,
face, sights.

Now the gramophone sulks
in our house.
Our anger is round

with no grooves to land on.

Each poison   poised
in the very best mouth

and near begins our silences.

Cold Waltzes

Twirled down the years
dizzying the sleet,
our fingers blue and touching.

No music thawed
the arctic smile—
that gash our faces wore.

Were quill stiff spines
in the ballroom world,
ah, such cold waltzes.

Ozark Love

Cables in the grass—
messages from Tennessee
of honeystones and butterchurns
while daylight cranks my skin
on its gramophone. West of Natchez,
Missouri hills, the circling music.

Lodgepole pine and heliotrope
stippling the wind with seed
to reel Virginia, Arkansas;
Kentuckiana pure-bred fillies
jarring the 5-string banjo hills
in the Ozark summer.

My body feels like an Ozark banjo
twanged by the sun.
Lobelias snare the song and blueness
planned in every seed
deepens to another key
I hardly see and cannot turn:
a depth of music in the buried world.

Beyond Our Thirst

Too parched for words,
necks protruding
from our shell house,

(that heavy self
we had to drag),

we lost our gauge
of water.

Miles of silence
inched across,
our mouths fried brown

and crusted;
we came upon
a dune lip

and saw the water
split like quartz,

a broken quarry
beyond our thirst.

Unaware That Avessek

Berries on the outwash plain,
mudflat, esker, hole
and swamp
enclose the summer
he clings to
like a dozing lemur
in the croft of a tree.

Wrinkling the image
of drenched pines,
their peaks in the river,
he leaps
in the water,

unaware that Avessek,
Pharaoh of the North,
commands the ice
to go southward,

that,
outmost at the Arctic Pole,
cold sabres gash
a trembling sun.

Drumlins, Tarns and Eskers

He said I felt
like drumlins looked,
oval hills of glacial drift,
only warmer; in the rise and fall
like the landscape
on the outskirts
of Buffalo.

I said he laughed
like an alpine tarn,
crevasse of water
ringed by stones,
only louder; in the steepness
like the coning
of the Matterhorn.

Together we lived
like an esker,
ridge of gravel
lodged in ice,
only colder; like the crested
penguin emperor
in our scope of frost.

Smooth Holster,
Pistol-Smoke Blue Eyes

Your smooth holster,
pistol-smoke blue eyes,
bullskin fingers ripping
my camisole of whalebone.

Night roped in the room,
gagged and spurting dirt.
Moon strung on the Gambel oak
slackening at dawn.

Bent to crooked hoops,
circles that your haunches rode.
Noose around my tongue,
silence that my refuge took.

Cordovan mustang, the morning charged,
bolted to the water trough.
I stroked its dazzled mane,
swilling kisses in my mouth.

Bells of St. Basil

The speed below our limitations,
we never went express, except once on the mattress
unsnapping my dress, my breath's propeller turboprop.
The fullest chafing inside my wish,
a clanging darkness, our powerhouse.

Your bones mounting mine,
I, the plateau and you, the Tanganyikan sky bearing down,
primate grunts and baboon refinements, the tacky room
widening continents of heat, your hair the baboon's coat
pressed to my face. We raided our bodies for stalks and fruit,

and in my mind I tore off my skin, gave you the miles
my intestines ran. Impasse of bones? I cracked them at the joint.
Here, love, my tibia for your soup, my ulna for your dog,
my heart for a stew to keep you warm.

Cold days in Normandy pinned to your eyes
surveying my orphanhood spread on the bed.
You huffed in a shrug, semen intact;
the Bells of St. Basil like musical knives
stabbing the dawn.

Seraphina

I saw her shoulder bloom,
SHAZAM,
along the runnel of the shore
and crumbled at her naked glaze,
her salt mouth kissing my summer.

Instructions for the Erection
of a Statue of Myself in Central Park

Let me be formed with stone;
a slab of diorite between my ears
will do for brains,
a round cut ruby for a heart.

Breasts? Alabaster mounds
that will not sag from suckling time,
against which birds will bat their wings
and rain will stroke and wind . . .

Cold to sex, and blood, and birth,
drape my marble thighs with snow.
Then let the lovers, hot with quarreling and tears,
stand in my shadow and kiss.